The Man with Two Shadows and Other Ghost Stories

MARK LEMON, JOSEPH SHERIDAN LE FANU,
TOM HOOD and CATHERINE CROWE

Level 3

Retold by Louise Greenwood
Series Editors: Andy Hopkins and Jocelyn Potter

Pearson Education Limited
Edinburgh Gate, Harlow,
Essex CM20 2JE, England
and Associated Companies throughout the world.

ISBN: 978-1-4058-8193-7

'The Dead Man of Varley Grange' was first published in 1878, 'The Ghost
Detective' was first published in 1866, 'The Dream' was first published in 1838,
'The Man with Two Shadows' from *The Shadow of a Shade* was first
published in 1869, 'The Ghost in the Bank of England' was first published
in 1879 and 'The Italian's Story' was first published in 1859
This adaptation first published by Penguin Books Ltd 1993
Published by Addison Wesley Longman Ltd and Penguin Books Ltd 1998
New edition first published 1999
This edition first published 2008

3 5 7 9 10 8 6 4 2

Text copyright © Louise Greenwood 1993
Illustrations copyright © David Cuzik 1993

The moral right of the adapter and of the illustrator has been asserted

Typeset by Graphicraft Ltd, Hong Kong
Set in 11/14pt Bembo
Printed in China
SWTC/02

Published by Pearson Education Ltd in association with
Penguin Books Ltd, both companies being subsidiaries of Pearson Plc

For a complete list of the titles available in the Penguin Readers series please write to your local
Pearson Longman office or to: Penguin Readers Marketing Department, Pearson Education,
Edinburgh Gate, Harlow, Essex CM20 2JE, England.

Contents

Introduction

Everyone went silent. Then one of the men picked up his gun and shot at it, but nothing happened. The thing just smiled . . .

Do you want to know about ghosts? There are many kinds. There are ghosts who tell people about death and danger. You'll meet them when you read about the old man of the Bank of England, and the thin, white man of Varley Grange. There are ghosts who punish bad people. Pat Connell, in 'The Dream', learns that the hard way. Some ghosts come back to find or finish something. A murdered sailor can't rest until he finds his murderer. There are ghosts of people who can never rest. Why? Because of the terrible things that they did in life, like Jacopo Ferraldi in 'The Italian's Story'. There are ghosts of living men too – men in prison for crimes that they did not do. And men who see terrible things and ghosts before they die . . .

In these six stories you will meet all these, and more. Now, do you *really* want to know about ghosts?

Ghost stories were much more popular in the 1800s than in the 1700s. In the 1700s, many people thought that science and reason could explain everything. In this 'age of reason', they were not very excited by things like dreams or ghosts.

Then, at the beginning of the 1800s, people became bored with amusing and clever stories about real life. They wanted stories about things that science and reason could not explain. Stories about strange, foreign countries became popular, stories about ghosts in big, dark houses and mysterious animals in shadowy forests; stories about brave young men who saved beautiful young women from death and terrible danger. People wanted stories to frighten them.

These stories are called 'Gothic' stories. Three of the most popular early Gothic stories from that time are Mary Shelley's *Frankenstein* (1818), John Polidori's *The Vampyre* (1819), and Sir Walter Scott's *Three Tales of Terror* (1824–28).

Then, in the middle of the 1800s, the ghost story changed. Ghosts moved out of large, dark houses in foreign lands, and moved into ordinary houses in everyday life. Ghosts walked along streets and around gardens, and they came through windows into ordinary homes. Nobody was safe. It was easier to believe in ghosts, and they became even more frightening.

Charles Dickens (1812–70) wrote many ghost stories. Two of his most famous are *A Christmas Carol* (1852) and *The Signalman* (1866). He liked ghost stories so much that he started a magazine for them in 1859. Many famous writers wrote for this magazine, for example Wilkie Collins, Elizabeth Gaskell, Mark Lemon and Joseph Sheridan Le Fanu. Le Fanu's stories were unusual because his ghosts were often not just in a room, but inside a person's head.

Towards the end of the 1800s, ghost story writers followed Le Fanu's example more and more. They became interested in questions like: When does a man stop being a man? When does he start to become something different? This was the most frightening kind of story of all. It was impossible to escape from the ghost or the thing inside your head, because it lived inside you. It used your body and blood and ate your heart and mind, and you went crazy.

The most famous books of this type were Robert Louis Stevenson's *Dr Jekyll and Mr Hyde* (1886), Oscar Wilde's *The Picture of Dorian Gray* (1891), and Bram Stoker's *Dracula* (1897). All three are Penguin Readers.

The stories in this book are from the middle of the 1800s, at the time when ghost stories took place in everyday life.

Joseph Sheridan Le Fanu (1814–73) was born in Dublin, Ireland, and studied at Trinity College, Dublin. He worked for newspapers for many years. After his wife died, he stayed at home and saw few people. He wrote over 20 books, but he is best known for his clever ghost stories. His books *House by the Churchyard* (1863), *Uncle Silas* (1864) and his book of short stories *In a Glass Darkly* (1872) have some of the most frightening stories in the English language.

Mark Lemon (1809–70) was a businessman before he became a writer. He wrote songs, Christmas stories and joke books, but most of his writing was for the theatre. In 1851 he wrote a short, funny play with Charles Dickens called *Mr Nightingale's Diary*, and they acted in it together. He is most famous for starting the British magazine *Punch*.

Tom Hood (1835–74) was the son of the famous writer, Thomas Hood. Like his father, he wrote poems, but he is mostly famous for his amusing writing. He wrote for newspapers and wrote many children's books, often working with his sister. He also drew the pictures for many of his books.

Catherine Crowe (1800–76) was born in the south of England but lived in Edinburgh, Scotland, for many years. Her real name was Catherine Stevens. She wrote a lot of children's books and other stories, but her most popular book was a book of ghost stories, *The Night Side of Nature* (1848).

Two of the stories in this book are anonymous. This means that the writer's name is not known.

People either believe in ghosts or they do not. But these are well written stories which everyone can enjoy. The next time you hear a strange noise or see a strange shape in the night, do not be afraid . . . it's probably only a ghost!

The Dead Man of Varley Grange

Anonymous, 1878

'Hallo, Jack. Where are you going? Are you staying with your parents for Christmas?' Jack Darent and I were in the army together. It was December the 23rd and everyone was going away for the holiday.

Jack stood in the doorway, tall and good-looking, laughing at my question. 'Not this year. I've had enough of old aunts and my sister's six children. I'm not a family man like you. By the way, how is your beautiful sister?'

'She's very well and going to lots of parties,' I answered, smiling.

Jack looked a little sad at this. He was in love with my sister and she was in love with him, but they did not have enough money to get married. 'Well, please send her my love,' he said. 'I'm going down to your part of England – Westernshire – for some shooting. Henderson has asked me and some others. We're staying in an old house, where I hear the shooting is very good. Perhaps you know it? It's called Varley Grange.'

'Varley Grange?' I said. 'Oh no, Jack. You can't go there.'

'Why not?' he asked, surprised.

'I've heard . . . uncomfortable things about that house,' I said, searching for the right words.

'Uncomfortable? What do you mean?' laughed Jack. 'It'll probably be a bit cold and there'll be a few rats maybe, but Henderson's French cook is coming and he's bringing lots of wine. I'm sure I won't feel the cold.'

'No, Jack. I don't think you quite understand . . .' I began. I think he thought I was a bit crazy.

1

'Well, I must go, or I'll miss the train. See you after Christmas,' he said happily, not hearing my last words, and he was gone.

When I got home, my wife, my sister Bella, and my two children were all waiting for me to have tea.

'I've just seen Jack Darent, Bella,' I said.

'Oh yes,' she answered, pretending not to be interested. 'And where's he going for Christmas?'

'You'll be surprised when I tell you. He's going to Varley Grange.'

'Varley Grange?' she said. 'But that's terrible! Did you try to stop him?'

'Of course I did, but he didn't understand.'

She did not wait to hear any more, but ran out of the room, crying.

My wife was very confused. She was from London, not Westernshire, and she did not know the story of Varley Grange. 'Why is she crying?' she asked. 'What is this place you're talking about?'

'Well, my dear, do you believe in ghosts?' I asked her.

'Of course not,' she said, looking at the children, who were listening carefully. 'Wait, let me take the children out.'

When the children were playing happily in another room, I told her the story. 'Varley Grange is an old house in Westernshire. It belonged to the Varley family – all of them are dead now. The last two members of the family, Dennis Varley and his sister, lived there a hundred years ago. The sister fell in love with a poor man and her brother didn't want them to marry. To stop them, he locked her up. One night she and her lover ran away, but her brother caught her and took her back to Varley Grange, where he killed her.'

'He murdered his own sister?'

'Yes. And since that day, Dennis Varley's ghost has walked around the house. Many people have seen it. They say that if you

Bella did not wait to hear any more, but ran out of the room, crying.

also see the ghost of his sister, you will have very bad luck or a serious illness, or perhaps you'll even die.'

Of course, my wife did not believe the story and we all forgot about it until a week later when I saw Jack again, sitting in a London café.

'Well, Jack, how was the shooting?' I asked. From his white face I saw that all was not well. He asked me to sit down.

'I understand now what you were saying before I left London,' he began. 'I'm only sorry I didn't listen to you.'

'Did you see something?' I asked.

'I saw everything,' he whispered. 'Let me tell you what happened. We all left London together and had a good journey down to Westernshire. We were all very happy and that night we slept well. The next day, we went shooting. It was wonderful — birds everywhere. We shot about two hundred altogether, and

Henderson's French cook made us a wonderful dinner from them. After the food we all sat around drinking coffee, smoking and telling stories about shooting and fishing. Suddenly one of us – I can't remember who it was – shouted and pointed up to the top of the stairs. We all looked round and there was a man looking down at us.'

'How was he dressed?' I asked.

'He was wearing black clothes, but it was his face that I noticed most. It was white and thin and he had a long beard and terrible eyes. He looked like a dead man. As we watched he went into my bedroom and everyone ran to the stairs. We searched all the rooms but could find nothing.

'Well, none of us slept very well that night, but the next morning at breakfast, Henderson asked us not to talk about it any more. He seemed quite angry and did not want the servants to hear. We had another good day's shooting and we all slept well that night. Two nights went by and nothing happened. Then, on the third night, we were sitting by the fire after dinner as before, when suddenly the room went cold. I knew it was there before I turned and saw it at the top of the stairs. Everyone went silent. Then one of the men picked up his gun and shot at it, but nothing happened. The thing just smiled and, once again, went into my bedroom.

'The next morning, four out of the eight of us decided to leave immediately. Some said they had important business in London, others suddenly remembered that they had to see their families. Anyway, there were four of us left – Wells, Harford, Henderson and myself. In the morning, we were all happy and laughing about the ghost and we decided that someone from the village was probably making fools of us. Henderson told us the story he heard from one of the villagers about Dennis Varley's murder of his sister. I'm sure you know it, so I won't tell you again.'

'We saw the dead man coming slowly up the stairs.'

'Yes, I do know it,' I said. 'I also know that anyone who sees the ghosts of both Dennis and his sister will have terrible bad luck.'

'Not only that,' said Jack. 'Anyone who sees the sister's face will die within one year.' His face turned whiter as he said this and he did not speak for a few minutes. Then he continued his story.

'Well, that night we felt far less brave than in the morning. At eleven o'clock we all waited in different places for the ghosts to come. I was at the top of the stairs with Harford opposite me. There was a storm outside and the wind made a sound like someone crying. At midnight there was a scream from Henderson downstairs and Harford and I jumped up. We saw the dead man coming slowly up the stairs towards us. Henderson ran after it and, as the ghost passed us, we felt cold and terribly afraid.

Then, suddenly, Harford held my arm and pointed. I turned and saw the ghost of the sister coming. She wore a long, black and white dress and she had a big cross round her neck. I could not see her face, but I wanted to – I don't know why, I couldn't stop myself. I went towards her and, as I did so, she looked up.'

'You saw her face? What was it like?' I asked.

'I saw it,' he said, 'but I can never describe it to anyone.'

'Well, what happened next?' I asked.

'I can't remember. I think I fell. Everything just went black. I left the house the next day. I know that I'll die in a year and something terrible will happen to Harford. He saw her too, but not her face. The others only saw the brother.'

I decided not to tell my sister the terrible story, but soon things happened which everyone heard about. Bob Harford's wife ran away from him two days after they got married. He has gone to live in a wild part of Canada and no one hears from him any more. And Jack Darent? Poor, handsome Jack Darent died in South Africa about eleven months after I met him in the café that day. And my sister Bella? She is still beautiful, but she always wears black and she always looks sad.

The Ghost Detective

Mark Lemon, 1866

When I first came to London thirty years ago, I met a young man, James Loxley, who worked in the wine business. The company he worked for sold wine to pubs and restaurants, and just after I met him he got a new job in the company with more money. Because of this he was able to get married and I went to his wedding. His wife was a pretty girl with fair hair and blue eyes. It was clear to everyone that they loved each other.

They went to live in a new house outside London and I visited them often. Over the next three years, they had two beautiful children and they were a very happy family. They did not have much money and had only one servant, a rather stupid girl called Susan. One year they asked me to come to their home for Christmas dinner. We had a lovely meal and then sat in their sitting-room, laughing and talking. It was a small but comfortable room. In the corner was a Christmas tree and on the wall was a painting of Loxley's mother and father, who were both dead. Loxley loved this painting. He told me that it was just like his parents and he often felt that they were really in the room with him.

After Christmas Loxley came with me to visit my old uncle for a few days. He seemed very quiet during the trip and I thought perhaps he wanted to be with his wife and children. When the holiday was over, we travelled to London together early in the morning to go to work. He seemed worried during the journey but he did not say why. The next day I could not believe it when I heard that he was in prison for stealing money from his company. I immediately went to see him and on the way I remembered his quietness over the last few days. I also began to think about how expensive it was with two children and how Loxley probably needed money. But, no, it was impossible. I knew that he was an honest man.

At the prison I talked to him and this is the story he told me:

'On December the 24th, Christmas Eve, I went to one of my customers, John Rogers, and asked him to pay his bill. He is often late with payments and I wanted to get the money before the Christmas holiday. He gave me a cheque and I immediately took it to the bank and cashed it, because in the past this customer has written a cheque and then stopped it before we could get the cash. It was too late to go to the office, so I decided to keep the money until after the holiday. I put it in my pocket and went

Loxley told me that it was just like his parents and he often felt that
they were really in the room with him.

home. On the day we left my house to visit your uncle, I could not find the money and I became very worried. I looked all over the house, but it was nowhere. I was afraid to go back to work. When I told my boss about it, he did not understand why I didn't come to the office immediately when I couldn't find the money. He did not believe my story and called me a thief.'

At that moment we heard someone crying and screaming outside the door. It was Loxley's wife, Martha. She ran in, held her husband in her arms and cried and cried. It was terrible to see. After some time the prison guard told us to leave, and I took her home, still crying. She became ill and her mother came to stay with her and the children. The servant, Susan, was also there. She seemed to be a good girl and was always ready to help, but she seemed very unhappy about the problem and sometimes cried more than Martha. I visited the little house almost every day and, one day, I found Martha very excited.

'What's happened, Martha?' I asked.

'Well, you probably won't believe this,' she said, 'but last night I saw my husband's ghost.'

'But James isn't dead,' I said, 'he's only in prison.'

'I know, I know,' she said, 'but listen to this. Last night at midnight I was in the sitting-room – I couldn't sleep as usual. I was sitting worrying about our problems. Suddenly I looked up and saw James come into the room without a sound. He sat down over there in his favourite chair and looked at the picture of his father for a few minutes without speaking. Then he stood up and looked at me with a face full of love and walked out of the room.'

'Perhaps you were half asleep and dreamed it,' I said, but she was sure about what happened and did not want to listen to me.

Susan, the servant girl, was in the room with us and was listening to the conversation, looking very afraid. 'Did you speak to the ghost, Mrs Loxley? Did it say anything to you?' she asked.

'No, Susan. I've told you everything that happened,' said Martha.

I left the house that day feeling very worried as Martha was looking so white and tired. I thought about calling a doctor, but I decided to wait and see what happened. The next day I visited them again and found Martha even more excited.

'He came again,' she almost shouted. 'This time he stood in front of the painting of his father and pointed at it. Then he turned to me and held out his arms. I ran towards him, but he disappeared and I crashed into the wall. I think he means there is something behind the picture. Please, will you help me to take it down and look?'

The painting was quite high on the wall and I needed a ladder to reach it. I called Susan and asked her to bring one.

'This time James stood in front of the painting of his father and pointed at it.'

'A ladder?' she asked. 'What for?'

When I explained about the painting I was surprised to see her face turn white. 'There isn't a ladder,' she said quickly.

'But I'm sure I saw one,' I said, 'just outside the kitchen door. Oh well, my mistake. Don't worry.'

Susan didn't leave the room but watched as I stood on a chair and began to take the picture of Loxley's father down. Suddenly she screamed, 'It was me, Mrs Loxley. I know why the ghost came. The money's behind the picture. I hid it there.' She began to cry and cry, and it was some time before she could tell the story.

'It was on Christmas Eve,' she said. 'Mr Loxley came home a bit late. I was behind him as he was walking upstairs, and he took his handkerchief out of his pocket. As he did so, the money fell out. He didn't notice, but I did and I picked it up. It was more money than I've seen in my life, Mrs Loxley, I couldn't stop myself. Then I was frightened about someone finding it on me or in my room, so I hid it behind that picture. Oh, please Mrs Loxley. Don't send me to prison.'

Well, as soon as Susan told her story to the police, James was a free man, and the family are now living happily in Australia.

The Dream

Joseph Sheridan Le Fanu, 1838

In the year 1750 I was working at the church in Castleton, a small town in the south of England. One night a knock at the door woke me up. Outside was a poor little girl, crying loudly. After a few minutes, I understood that her father was very ill, almost dying, and she wanted me to come to him.

'Of course I'll come,' I said. 'Where do you live? Who is your father?' She did not answer but began to cry more loudly. Again I

11

waited until she was calm, and then asked her the same question.

'My father is Pat Connell,' she said, 'and now I'm sure that you won't come.'

I knew about Pat Connell. He was a bad man, who often stole things, and he drank too much beer. I never saw him in church. He was a bad man, but he was dying and I had to go to him, to say a few words to help him as he died.

I put on my coat and followed the poor little girl through the cold, dark streets. We walked quickly and our way took us to the worst part of the town. The streets were narrow, the houses were old and there was a terrible smell. The girl went through a small door and I followed her up the broken stairs to the top of the building. She took me up to the bedroom where her father lay. His wife and children were sitting round the bed watching worriedly. The doctor was also with him. I went closer to the man and looked at his face, which was blue from too much drink. His lips were black and, from his breathing, I felt sure that death was not far away.

'Is there any hope?' I asked the doctor. He shook his head and listened to the man's heart.

'This man is dead,' he said, and turned away from the bed.

The wife and children began to cry. I stood still, watching them, feeling sad that I was too late to help the dead man, too late to talk to him about God.

Suddenly the wife screamed and pointed at the bed. I turned round quickly and saw the body of the man sitting up in bed. For a few seconds I could not move. I stood, confused, thinking of dead men and ghosts until I realized that the man was alive. The doctor ran to look at him and found blood running from a cut in the man's body.

'The blood coming out has made him better,' he said. 'I've never seen this before. He's very lucky.'

The doctor and the man's wife made him comfortable, and I

I turned round quickly and saw the body of the man sitting up in bed.

left, promising to return the next day. I did go back the next day and the day after, but the sick man was always sleeping. On the third day I returned and found him awake. As I went in, he shouted, 'Oh, thank you, thank you for coming. I want to talk to you.' I sat down next to the bed and he began to talk.

'I've been a very bad man, I know that,' he said. 'I've stolen, I've drunk too much, I've had a bad life, but I don't want to go to hell.' He began to cry and could not stop for some time. I gave him a glass of water and he continued. 'I must tell you what happened that night you came here. I know you'll understand as a man of the church. I came in late after drinking a lot of beer. I went to bed but woke up a few hours later. I wanted to get some air but I didn't want to wake the children by opening the window, so I started to go downstairs. As it was very dark I counted the stairs so that I did not fall at the bottom. Well, I got to the bottom of the first stairs, but suddenly the floor broke under me and I started to fall.

'I fell and fell for a long time through the blackness and when I stopped I was at a big table. Sitting at the table were lots of men. There was a smell of fire all around and the light was red. Suddenly, I realized that I was in hell. I was dead. I opened my mouth to scream, but no sound came out. I tried to stand up. I wanted to run away, but the man sitting next to me put his hand on my shoulder. "Sit down, my friend. You can *never* leave this place," he said. His voice was weak, like a child's. Then at the end of the table the tallest of the men stood up. I felt that he was able to control me; he seemed very strong, and he had such a terrible face. He pointed at me with his long, black finger. "You can leave now," he said in a frightening voice, "but you must promise to come back in three months' time." I shouted, "I promise to come back, but in God's name let me go now." The next thing I knew I was sitting up in bed and the doctor was there. Oh, please tell me, was it hell? Did I go to hell or was it just a terrible dream? I don't want to go back.'

I thought carefully, and then I said, 'Pat, I'm sure it was a dream, which you felt strongly because you were ill, but it is also a warning to you. Only bad people go to hell. If you live a good life from now, if you stop drinking and stealing and come to church, you will not go back down there.'

When I left he was looking much happier. A few days later, I visited the house again and found him much better. He was mending the floor at the bottom of the first stairs. 'This was where I went through. I just want to be safe,' he explained.

For several weeks Pat Connell was a different man. He stopped drinking and stealing, he worked hard to look after his family, and he came to church every Sunday. One day I met him in the street, coming home from work. We spoke a few words and when I left him he looked happy and well. But a few days later, he was dead.

'When I woke up, I saw two people going silently out of the room.'

I went to see his wife and she told me what happened. 'Pat was doing so well. I was proud of the way he stopped drinking, but one night he met an old friend, just returned from the army. He was so pleased to see him that, without thinking, he went into the pub with this friend. Well, of course, they started drinking, and one beer followed another. His friends had to carry him home and we all put him in his bed. I stayed down here by the fire. I was feeling sad, thinking about all our problems. I think I fell asleep for a few minutes. When I woke up, I saw two people, one of them my husband, Pat, going silently out of the room. I called to him, "Pat, where are you going?" but he didn't answer me. The door closed. Then I heard a terrible crash from above. I ran up the first stairs and there was Pat. He was dead – his back was broken. I think he was coming down from the bedroom when he fell at the bottom of the first stairs, you know, the place he was mending when you came to visit.'

I remembered the place well. The place which, in Pat's dream, was the entrance to hell. The place where he knew he had to go back.

The Man with Two Shadows

from The Shadow of a Shade, *Tom Hood, 1869*

My sister Lettie had lived with me ever since I got married. She is my wife's best friend and my children all love her, but her face is always sad. Many men have asked her to marry them but she has always said no, since she lost her first real love.

George Mason was my wife's cousin, a sailor. He and Lettie met at our wedding and fell in love immediately. George was a brave man, who loved the sea, and I was not surprised when he decided to travel to the Arctic on a ship called the *Pioneer*. Lettie was afraid when he told her, but she could not stop him. I knew that she was worried because, for the first time in her life, she began to look sad sometimes.

My younger brother Harry liked painting, so he decided to paint a picture of George before he left. It was quite a good picture. I thought the face was too white but Lettie was very pleased with it and she put it on the wall in our sitting-room.

Before the ship sailed, George met the ship's doctor, a Scotsman called Vincent Grieve. He brought him to dinner with us and I disliked him immediately. He was a tall, thin man with fair hair and cold, grey eyes. His face looked hard and I felt sure that he was not honest. He sat too close to Lettie and seemed more like her lover than George. At first George did not notice, but Lettie did and she was unhappy about it. The strangest thing was when he saw the picture of George on the wall. He sat down opposite it, but stood up as soon as he saw it. 'I'm sorry,' he said, 'but I cannot look at that picture.'

'Well, I know it's not very good . . .' I began.

'It's not that it's either good or bad. I know nothing about painting,' he said. 'It's the eyes . . . they seem to follow me everywhere.'

I thought that perhaps he just wanted to move closer to Lettie, but when I saw his face, he looked really quite frightened.

At the end of the evening I quietly asked George about Vincent Grieve. 'Do you want to bring him to dinner again?' I whispered.

'No,' he answered. 'He's a good friend on the ship, but I don't like the way he is with ladies.'

We were all surprised when Vincent came again the next day. He brought a note for Lettie from George and after that he came almost every day. George was busier than him and did not have so much time to see Lettie. On the last day before the ship sailed, Vincent said to Lettie, 'If anything happens to George, I will still love you and you can marry me.'

Vincent Grieve said, 'It's the eyes . . . they seem to follow me everywhere.'

Lettie was very angry and told him to leave the house at once. She did not tell George about it because she wanted him to leave happily. The time came for George and Lettie to say goodbye and, when he left, Lettie cried for hours. I went in and put my arm around her. As I looked up, I noticed the picture of George on the wall. The face looked very, very white and I thought there was water on it. Perhaps it's just the light, I thought to myself and tried to forget about it.

The *Pioneer* sailed. George sent two letters, and then a year passed before we heard anything. We once read about the ship in the newspaper, but that was all. Spring-time came, and one beautiful warm evening we were all at home. The children were playing outside and Harry was watching them from the window. Suddenly the room felt very cold. Lettie looked up. 'How strange,' she said. 'Do you feel how cold it is?'

'Just like the weather in the Arctic,' I said. As I spoke, I looked at the picture on the wall and what I saw made me terribly afraid. His face suddenly looked like a dead man's, with no eyes. Without thinking, I said 'Poor George.'

'What do you mean?' asked Lettie, looking frightened. 'Have you heard something about George?'

'No, no,' I said quickly. 'I was just thinking about the cold weather where he is.'

At this moment, Harry put his head back into the room. 'Cold?' he said. 'Who's cold?'

'Did you not feel cold just then?' asked Lettie. 'We both did.'

'Not at all,' he said happily. 'How can you feel cold on a beautiful spring evening like this?'

I followed him out of the room. 'Harry,' I said, 'what's the date today?'

'It's Tuesday, February the 23rd. Look, here's the newspaper.'

I told him about the change in the picture and the cold feeling and asked him to write it down. I was sure that George was in some kind of trouble and I wanted to remember everything about that evening.

Later Lettie went to bed with a terrible cold and was ill all through the night. My wife was angry with me for sitting with the windows open and making my sister ill.

Early the next morning there was a knock at the door. It was Harry, looking white and frightened. I knew immediately why he was there.

'Have you seen the newspaper?' he asked.

On the front page was the news that George was dead. One sentence from the newspaper stayed in my mind: 'Lieutenant George Mason was out shooting with the ship's doctor, Vincent Grieve, when he died.'

When I told my wife about George, she began to cry. 'How can we tell poor Lettie?' she said.

'Ssssshh,' said Harry, but it was too late. Lettie was at the door and we had to tell her everything. She fell to the floor, her face as white as paper. We called the doctor immediately, but she was ill for many months.

About two months later, I read about the arrival of the *Pioneer*, George's ship, in Britain. I did not tell Lettie about it as she was only just getting better. A day or two after this there was a knock at the door and, as I got up to open it, I noticed George's picture once again. This time, to my surprise, he held one finger up and seemed to be warning me. I looked harder at George's face and was almost sure that I could see blood on it. I walked closer and saw that the warning finger was really a small moth, sitting on the picture. I picked up the sleepy moth and put

I walked closer and saw that the warning finger was really a small moth.

it under a wineglass. As I did this, the servant came in and said, 'Dr Vincent Grieve is here to see you, sir.'

As the doctor came in, I saw his face turn white. 'Please, cover that picture of George,' he said. 'It is even harder for me to look at it now that he is dead.'

I covered the picture and Grieve sat down. He looked very thin and white and, again, I felt a strong dislike for him. I asked him about the day George died and he told me the story.

'We were out shooting on the ice,' he said. 'It was not easy to walk. Suddenly, George fell. I tried to catch him . . . I threw my coat for him . . . I wanted to pull him up, but it was impossible. He fell into the ice-cold sea and slowly his head went under. His last words were "Say goodbye to her".'

As he finished his story, Grieve looked up. He screamed loudly and jumped up, pointing behind me. I looked round. The picture was uncovered again and George's white face looked down on us. I covered it again and Grieve seemed to feel better.

'I'm so sorry,' he said, 'I've been ill.' He stood up. 'I'm sorry,' he said again. Then he noticed the little white moth, which was still under the wineglass. 'Has someone else from the *Pioneer* been here?' he asked.

'No,' I answered. 'You are the first.'

'Then how did this moth get here? It only lives in the Arctic. That's very strange . . . Well, look after it. It's very unusual.'

He left a few minutes later and Harry and I watched him walk down the street. 'There's something I don't like about that man,' I said.

'You're right,' Harry said. 'Do you know he has two shadows? There's someone or something always standing at his side. That explains why he's always so frightened.'

We decided not to tell Lettie about his visit.

Two days later, I arrived home and found my sister very angry. 'Grieve came here today and asked me to marry him. He said that George wanted it. I couldn't believe it. We were in the sitting-room and he was standing by the wall. As he was speaking, there was a sound of something breaking, and George's picture fell on his head and cut it open. We had to carry him upstairs and call the doctor.'

I went angrily upstairs but, when I saw Grieve, it was clear that he could understand nothing. We could not move him and a nurse came to stay with him during the night. At about midnight, the nurse felt something was wrong in the room. She saw his two shadows on the wall and, frightened, went to get Lettie to sit with her. As soon as my sister came into the room, Grieve sat up and started to talk. 'I could not stop myself,' he said. 'I hit you with my gun because I loved her and now she'll never forgive me. I murdered you, George, because I loved her. Don't you see? Can't you understand? Please, please leave me alone.' As he shouted the last words, he got out of bed and walked backwards slowly, all the time looking at something following him, his eyes wide and afraid. He came to the window and suddenly seemed to decide something. Very quickly, he turned round, and Lettie could not stop him. Two days later, the police found his body in the river.

Now the picture of George is always covered. It has not changed again. Only Lettie's face has changed – she never laughs or smiles now.

The Ghost in the Bank of England

Anonymous, 1879

1

Many stories end with a wedding. Mine begins with one. The day that I married Annie Burdon was one of the happiest of my life. Everyone said we were crazy. We had no money and I was a young doctor with no job, but we loved each other.

After the wedding we were very poor and I could not find a job. I tried everywhere until, one day, I found a job as a doctor on a ship, sailing to Jamaica. I did not want to leave Annie, but I was not able to choose – I had to get some money.

The name of the ship was the *Darien* and my boss was Mr Julius Mendez, a small man of about fifty years old. Nobody liked him and, after one day at sea, I began to feel the same. He thought about one thing only – his health. He came to see me two or three times a day, worried about his heart, his stomach, his head or some other part of his body.

When we arrived at Kingston in Jamaica, Mr Mendez came to see me and said, 'I'm not sure if you will believe this, but I am in danger of dying before the end of my fifty-seventh year. I will be fifty-eight on September the 10th, and after midnight on that day I will be safe and able to live a long life. I cannot explain why or how I know this, but believe me it is true. I am frightened of dying and I don't like the doctors here. Please will you stay with me as my doctor and look after me? I will pay you well and after midnight on September the 10th you will be free to leave.'

At the end of the first month he paid me £50, which I immediately sent to Annie. The second month seemed very long. I was with Mr Mendez all day and all night because he was so worried, but he was healthy all the time. At last September the 10th came and Mr Mendez did not die. He thanked me and gave me my money, which I sent to Annie. My plan was to leave Jamaica on the *Darien*, but I became ill and it was a long time before I could start my journey home.

2

I looked like a ghost when I arrived home many months later. Annie was living with her brother and all the family thought I was dead. I was so happy when I saw my family again, but soon I started to worry. I still had no job and I was weak after my illness in Jamaica. I looked for a job in an office – anything for money – but it was still impossible. I found nothing.

One day I was looking for a pen on Annie's desk, when I noticed a letter from Jamaica.

'Oh, yes. I forgot all about that letter,' said Annie, 'it arrived while you were away.'

I opened it and found a letter from Julius Mendez. The letter said.

September the 12th, 1832

Dear Wilson,
You probably thought it was strange that I did not really thank you for your work. I am sending you this cheque, which I hope will help you.

Yours faithfully,
Julius Mendez

With the letter was a cheque for £1,000! At first I thought I was dreaming. All these months we were poor and worried about money and the cheque was sitting on Annie's desk. We were so happy. I immediately wrote a letter of thanks to Mr Mendez and then decided to go to London the next day to

With the letter was a cheque for £1,000!

cash the cheque. I had to take it to the Bank of England.

On the journey I met Mr Deacon, one of our neighbours.

'Where are you going, young Wilson?' he asked.

'I have to go to the Bank of England,' I answered.

'Ah,' he said, smiling, 'do you know I worked there as a cashier for twenty years. I still remember my desk ... it was a lucky one. I haven't been back there for forty years.'

'A lucky desk?' I asked, surprised.

'Oh, yes,' he said, 'everyone in the bank knew that some desks were lucky and some were unlucky. Men who sat in some desks did very well and got better jobs, others ... well ... I can tell you about one unlucky desk as an example. A young man called Fred Hawes sat there. He was a good-looking, happy young man and he had a beautiful sister, Nancy who loved her brother very much. She worked hard to make more money for the family and she always looked after Fred. All the cashiers were in love with her and many young men, including myself, asked her to marry them, but she always said no. There was one young man, Isaac Ayscough, who was a close friend of Fred's. Nancy was frightened of him. She knew Isaac loved her but she only felt afraid of him and was always worried about Fred spending time with him. One day there was a problem at the bank. Some money disappeared and Isaac said that Fred was the thief. Fred went to prison and died there. Of course, his sister was very unhappy and became a little – well, odd. She came to the bank every day after Fred died and she always asked the same question, "Is my brother, Mr Frederick, here today?" and one of us always answered, "No, miss, not today." Then she always said, "Give my love to him when he returns and say I'll call tomorrow." One day she didn't come and we heard that she was dead.'

'And what about Isaac Ayscough?' I asked.

'Well,' continued Mr Deacon, 'after Fred's death, they moved him from a lucky desk to Fred's old, unlucky one. He came to work every day at the same time and left at the same time. He never spoke to anyone. He never married, but lived alone in a small room. He died suddenly at the age of fifty. Now they say that his ghost always comes to the bank when someone cashes the cheque of a dead man. Many people have seen it.'

As Mr Deacon finished his story, our journey ended and we said goodbye.

3

Soon I was walking in the busy streets of London. When I came to the Bank of England, I took the cheque from my pocket and looked at it again. I wanted to be sure it was real. I went into the bank and at first I felt confused. There were so many desks with

I went into the bank and at first I felt confused. There were so many desks with cashiers behind them.

cashiers behind them – I did not know which one to go to. Then I noticed one of the cashiers looking at me. He was older than the other cashiers and was standing behind them. His clothes looked odd, perhaps from some years ago, and his face looked strange – thin and white, like a dead man's. He had a red scar on his face in the shape of a letter Y. The other cashiers were busy, so I gave him my cheque. I took the £1,000 banknote from him and left the bank quickly, feeling uneasy. But I returned home a rich man.

4

Everything was wonderful for a year. I found a job and we lived well. I enjoyed my work as a doctor. Then one day I was surprised to find a man from the Bank of England and a policeman at my house. They asked lots of questions about my cheque and the £1,000 banknote. I answered them all and they left, but the next day they returned. They said that my £1,000 banknote was not real, and that night I found myself in prison. I could not believe it. How could the note not be real? The police asked me the same questions again, and again I gave the same answers. They asked me about the cheque from Mr Mendez.

'What was the date on the cheque, Mr Wilson?' asked the detective.

'It was the same date as the letter, September the 12th,' I answered. 'Look, here it is.'

'I think *you* wrote the letter and the cheque, Mr Wilson. Do you know why? We have heard from the police in Jamaica that Mr Mendez died on September the 11th. Now how do you think he wrote a letter and a cheque to you on the 12th? He was already dead. You say that you cashed the cheque at the Bank of England. The banknote is not a real one – how do you explain that? The number on it is not from the Bank of England. Perhaps you made it yourself?'

I was so confused I could not speak. How did Mr Mendez die on September the 11th? That was the day after I left him and the day before he wrote my cheque. It was impossible. All I knew was that I was not crazy and I was not a criminal. 'Take me to the Bank of England,' I said, 'and I will show you the cashier who took my cheque and gave me the £1,000 banknote.'

5

Mr Deacon, the man who travelled with me to London that day and told me the ghost story, heard about my troubles. He liked me and felt sorry for me, so he came to visit me in prison. 'I'll come with you and the detective to the bank, tomorrow,' he said. 'Perhaps I'll be able to help.'

We arrived at the bank early the next day. The detective told me to look carefully at all the cashiers. Of course, I could not see the strange older man in his odd clothes anywhere.

'He's not here,' I said quietly.

'I knew it – a waste of time,' said the detective angrily. 'Of course he's not here.'

Mr Deacon stopped him. 'Wait,' he said, 'can you describe the cashier?'

I told them about the man's strange, old clothes, his thin, white face and the red scar in the shape of a letter Y. 'He didn't look alive,' I said, 'he looked more like a dead man.'

'That's because he *was* dead,' said Mr Deacon. 'You saw the ghost of Isaac Ayscough. Do you remember the story I told you that day? Do you know that his ghost always comes when the cheque of a dead man is cashed? Ask any banker,' he said, turning to the detective. 'Ask anyone at the Bank of England or any bank in the country. They all know the story of the ghost in the Bank of England.'

The police asked hundreds of questions that day and they heard the same story from everyone in the bank. Finally, they had to believe it and in the evening I was a free man.

The Italian's Story

Catherine Crowe, 1859

This is the story of my family, the Ferraldis. It is a very old Italian family and my story begins in 1550, in Florence, which was an important business centre at that time. Jacopo Ferraldi was a very rich man. He kept all his money under the floor in his house and was only happy when he was counting it. He was always afraid of thieves and so he had no friends and only two servants. One day he found that £2,000 was missing. To him this was not a lot of money but he was very angry and told his servants to leave.

Not long after this, a letter arrived from his sister, who lived in England. In the letter she said that her husband was dead and that her son, Arthur Allen, was coming to Florence to try to make some money for the family, who were now very poor. Jacopo was angry. He did not want his nephew to come, but when the young man arrived his anger changed to happiness. The young man had £2,000 with him and Jacopo decided to steal it.

That night, while they were having dinner, Jacopo murdered his nephew and hid his body under the floor. He counted the money happily, but the next night, when he sat down to dinner, Jacopo saw the ghost of his nephew in the chair opposite him. This happened every night at dinner-time and he started to feel more and more uncomfortable.

He counted the money happily.

He decided that the only way to stop the ghost coming was to travel to England and pay back the £2,000 to his sister. Of course, he could not leave the rest of his money at home, so he put it all into big boxes and took it with him. After weeks of travelling, Jacopo arrived at his sister's house in England. Two servants carried his boxes into the house and from their heaviness they guessed that the boxes were full of money.

Jacopo gave £2,000 to his sister, but of course he told her nothing about her son's death. 'I'm afraid he never arrived in Florence,' he said. He did not see the ghost again, but his next worry was his money. He was sure that the servants were planning to steal it. He was right. That night they came to Jacopo's room, murdered him and took the boxes. The next morning, a neighbour found the empty boxes at the side of the road. The police searched the servants' rooms, but they found nothing. They questioned the servants, but it seemed that they really had no idea about the money. It was gone.

Two hundred and fifty years later, I, Francesco Ferraldi, was born in the house of Jacopo Ferraldi in Florence. As I grew up, I felt that it was an unhappy house, and when I was older, my parents told me the story of the murder of Arthur Allen. They were very ashamed of Jacopo Ferraldi and no one in the family ever said his name. Every time I went into the room where Jacopo killed his nephew and hid his body, I was sure I could hear strange cries and screams.

A few years later, because my family was poor, I travelled to England to try to make some money. I was a good singer, so I went to all the rich people's houses in London and sang at parties for money. At one of these parties, a kind old man, Mr Greathead, heard me and asked me to stay at his house in the country for the summer. 'I would like you to sing at all my parties and to give lessons to my daughters,' he said. I was very happy to agree.

When I arrived Mr Greathead showed me round the house and garden. When we came to the flower garden, I was surprised to see a small part of it covered in Italian flowers.

'How do they grow here?' I asked. 'I've never seen them outside Italy.'

'I think the ground is very rich here,' said Mr Greathead. 'But, funnily enough, my wife and I have a disagreement about this part of the garden. I would like to make the house bigger by building here, but my wife won't agree. She says she saw the ghost here once.'

That night at dinner I asked Mrs Greathead about the ghost in the flower garden. 'I really *did* see someone or something there,' she said. 'It was an old man. He was very thin and he was holding a pencil and paper. He was walking up and down between those Italian flowers and the tree. I got the idea that he was looking for something. I ran into the house but, of course, when my husband

'I really did *see someone or something there,'* Mrs Greathead said.

came out he could see no one. Some of the servants have seen him, they say, and the gardener says that, when he works in that part of the garden, the old man always appears. I've also heard stories of a murder here many years ago.'

Mr Greathead did not believe his wife's story and a few weeks later work began on that part of the garden. One of the men found an old coin and gave it to Mr Greathead, who showed it to me in great excitement.

'Look,' he said. 'It's in Italian, isn't it? And look at the date – 1545. How strange.'

The workmen found many more coins that day, and at dinner Mrs Greathead was very excited. 'You see,' she said to her husband, 'now you must believe me. All that money belonged to the old man I saw. Perhaps he hid it under the ground and then someone murdered him. Now his ghost is looking for the money.'

I began to think about Jacopo Ferraldi. Could it be? I thought. But no, it was impossible.

After dinner we had coffee in the library and I told the Greatheads my old family story about Jacopo and the murder of his nephew. As we talked I noticed something like a map, hanging on the wall. 'This looks very old,' I said. 'And . . . how strange . . . some of the words are in Italian.' As I looked closer I saw that it was in fact a map of the garden. I could see the flower garden and between the Italian flowers and the tree there was a cross. Mr Greathead came to look too.

'Yes,' he said, 'we think the gardens were designed by an Italian . . . but what's wrong?'

I was looking at the back of the map, where I saw the words 'Jacopo Ferraldi' and the date '1550'. Then I was sure. I was in the same house that the old murderer, Jacopo Ferraldi, came to all those years ago. The cross on the map showed the place where all his money was under the ground. I believe that he guessed the servants were planning to rob him, so he hid the money in the garden to keep it safe. His ghost has walked there ever since, guarding our family's money.

The Greatheads were very surprised and pleased, especially Mrs Greathead, who loved to be right. They were very happy to give all the old coins to me, which I sold for enough money to make me a very rich man.

ACTIVITIES

The Dead Man of Varley Grange

Before you read

1 Look at the Word List at the back of the book, and find:
   a three kinds of money
   b two words for feelings
   c three words for living people
   d one small living thing

2 Read the Introduction to the book and the title of the first story. Answer these questions.
   a How were ghosts different in English stories from:
     the early 1800s   the mid-1800s   the late 1800s
   b From which time are the stories in this book?
   c Do we know who wrote the first story?

While you read

3 Are these sentences true or not? Put *T* next to the true sentences.
   a Jack Darent loves his friend's sister, and she loves
     him.   .....
   b Henderson invites Jack to Varley Grange because
     the men enjoy shooting birds, eating and drinking.   .....
   c Bella laughs when she hears about Jack's visit to
     Varley Grange.   .....
   d Dennis Varley killed his sister in Varley Grange, and
     since then many people have seen his ghost there.   .....
   e People say that the murdered sister's ghost brings
     bad luck and perhaps death to people.   .....
   f The morning after Henderson's guests see the
     ghost with the long beard and terrible eyes, he tells
     his servants.   .....
   g Two ghosts appear at midnight, and Jack tries to
     see the face of the woman ghost.   .....
   h Jack knows he and Harford will die in a year.   .....

4 What happens to Harford, Jack Darent and Bella at the end of the story? Why?

5 Why do you think the sister's ghost shows her face only to Jack?

The Ghost Detective

Before you read

6 Look at the pictures in this story and answer these questions.
   a What season is it? How do you know?
   b What is the man pointing at in the second picture? How does the woman feel, do you think?

While you read

7 Complete sentences a–e. Write f–j after each one.
   a James Loxley loves the painting of his parents
      because ...   .
   b When Loxley goes to his uncle's house after
      Christmas, ...
   c The day after the two men travel to London, ...
   d John Rogers, one of Loxley's customers, pays
      Loxley with a cheque on December 24th, and ...   .
   e Loxley is very worried when he can't find the money ... .
   f he is very quiet during the trip.
   g Loxley cashes it immediately.
   h Loxley goes to prison for stealing money from his company.
   i but he doesn't tell his boss immediately.
   j he often feels they are really in the room with him.

8 What do you know about Loxley's wife, Martha? Tick (✓) the correct answers.
   a She visits her husband in prison and is angry with him.   .....
   b She has a servant, Susan, who cries very much about
      Mr Loxley.   .....

   c She tells the storyteller about the ghost, and Susan
     hears. .....

   d She asks the storyteller to destroy the painting of
     Loxley's parents because her husband's ghost
     pointed to it on his second visit. .....

   e She tells the police that her servant stole the money. .....

After you read

9 Work with another student. Have this conversation.

   Student A: You are James Loxley. Tell your boss about the money from John Rogers' cheque. Explain what happened.

   Student B: You are Loxley's boss and you do not believe him. Ask questions and tell him your plans.

10 Which people are dishonest in this story? What is the result of their dishonesty?

11 What is the most mysterious part of the story? Why?

The Dream

Before you read

12 Do you know any stories about dreams and ghosts? What do you think will happen in this story?

13 Why do ghost stories often happen at night, do you think?

While you read

14 Choose the best way to complete each sentence.

   a Pat Connell's daughter goes to the church because her father is ... .
     very ill   sorry for his bad life   dead

   b After the doctor says that Connell is dead, the dead man ... .
     screams   stands up   sits up

   c After Connell gets up and walks down the stairs, he ... .
     sits at his table   goes outside   falls through the floor

   d When Connell is in hell, he ... .
     screams loudly   wants to leave   cries

e Connell promises the tall man with the terrible face that he will ... .

live a better life   return to hell   control him

f After Connell goes drinking with his army friend, Connell's wife later sees her husband ... .

with somebody   in a dream   alone outside

After you read

15 Discuss with another student what happens to Connell at the end of the story. Why does it end this way, do you think?

16 Why are these things important to the story?

a beer   **b** the floor at the bottom of the first stairs   **c** dreams

The Man with Two Shadows

Before you read

17 The man in this story always has two shadows. How do you think this happens?

While you read

18 Underline the correct word in *italics*.

a Lettie, the storyteller's sister, and George Mason are lovers, but George also loves *the sea / painting*.

b The storyteller thinks that his brother's painting of George's face is too *dark / white*. But Lettie hangs it in the sitting-room.

c The storyteller dislikes Vincent Grieve, the ship's doctor, because he seems *strange / dishonest*.

d George Mason does not like Grieve sitting too near *the painting / Lettie*.

e One *warm / cold* spring evening, the sitting-room turns very cold, and the painting of George loses its colour and its eyes.

f George dies on February *23 / 24* while he is out shooting with Vincent Grieve.

g Immediately after the storyteller notices a moth and *a finger / some blood* on George's painting, Grieve arrives.

19 Write the missing word to complete these sentences.

    a After Grieve talks about George's death, he looks at the painting and ....

    b Harry tells .... that Grieve has two shadows.

    c Grieve asks Lettie to marry him. Then .... falls on Grieve's head and cuts it open.

    d Grieve tells George's shadow why he killed George. The shadow follows Grieve to the ....

After you read

20 Who says this to who and why?

    a 'It's the eyes ... they seem to follow me everywhere.'

    b 'Harry, what's the date today?'

    c 'How can we tell poor Lettie?'

    d 'Say goodbye to her.'

    e 'I murdered you, George, because I loved her.'

21 Discuss these questions.

    a Why is Grieve afraid of the painting?

    b How does the moth get into the storyteller's sitting-room, do you think?

    c Why does Grieve have two shadows?

The Ghost in the Bank of England

Before you read

22 Think about the title and answer these questions.

    a What do you think a ghost in a bank would want to do? Why?

    b Do you think this story happens at night or during the day?

While you read

23 Put these sentences in the correct order. Write 1–6.

    a Doctor Wilson finds a letter from Mendez dated September 12th with a cheque for £1,000. .....

    b He marries Annie Burdon but has no money and no job. .....

c Julius Mendez offers the doctor a lot of money if he
will look after him until midnight of his next birthday. .....

d On his way to the Bank of England with the cheque,
Doctor Wilson meets Mr Deacon, his neighbour,
who tells him about the lucky and unlucky desks
at the bank. .....

e After September 10th, Mendez is alive. So the doctor
is free, but he becomes very ill. .....

f The doctor accepts a job on a ship sailing to Jamaica. .....

24 Write the names of the people from the story.

a .... sat at an unlucky desk at the bank. **b** .... said he was a thief. After he died in prison, his sister **c** .... became a little odd. She asked to see her brother every day. Then **d** .... was moved to Fred's unlucky desk and he died suddenly at the age of fifty. In the story, **e** .... is sent to prison because his banknote from the cheque from **f** .... is not real. **g** .... describes the cashier at the Bank of England to the police – the dead cashier!

After you read

25 Why are these important in the story?

  a the *Darien* **b** September 10th
  c Mendez's letter **d** Fred's desk

26 Do you like the ending of this story? Why (not)?

The Italian's Story

Before you read

27 Look at the picture on page 31. When do you think this story happens? Where do you think this man keeps his money?

28 Describe the picture on page 33. What is the ghost doing, do you think?

29 One word in each sentence is wrong. Cross through the wrong word and write the correct word.

a When Jacopo Ferraldi finds that £2,000 of his money is missing, he sends his nephew away. ....

b After Jacopo murders his nephew, a woman visits his dinner table every night. ....

c Jacopo travels to England with all his money because he wants to return the £2,000 to Arthur's sister. ....

d Two hundred and fifty years after Jacopo is murdered by his sister's husband, Francesco Ferraldi is born in Jacopo's house in Italy. ....

e Francesco gets a job as a singer in Mr Greathead's house, and he is surprised to see a ghost in the garden. ....

After you read

30 What do you know about

a Jacopo Ferraldi and Arthur Allen?

b Jacopo's house and Francesco's house?

c the ghost and Jacopo Ferraldi?

31 Discuss these questions.

a Why does the ghost always appear when the gardener works near the Italian flowers?

b Why doesn't the ghost try to stop the workmen finding the coins?

c What do you think will happen to Francesco when he is rich?

Writing

32 Imagine you are Bob Harford in *The Dead Man of Varley Grange*. Write a letter from Canada to the newspaper in Westernshire. Explain why Varley Grange should be destroyed.

33 You are a reporter for the local newspaper. Loxley (in *The Ghost Detective*) is a free man again, and Susan is in prison. Write a short piece for the newspaper.

34 Write the conversation in *The Dream* between Connell and his old friend. Connell does not want to go back to his old life of heavy drinking. But his old friend says that just a few drinks won't matter.

35 Imagine you are Lettie in *The Man with Two Shadows*. You have discovered that Grieve killed George. Write in your daily notebook what you know about George's death.

36 Imagine you work for the London police. Write a report on the case of Mr Wilson, in *The Ghost in the Bank of England*, and the mysterious banknote. Explain why you had to free the doctor.

37 Imagine you are Francesco Ferraldi in *The Italian's Story*. The Greatheads have given you all the money. Write a letter to your parents in Florence. Tell them what has happened.

38 Compare two stories. In what ways are they similar? Which writer has written the most frightening story?

39 Imagine you have been asked to write a ghost story for a TV programme. Write a short description of your story.

40 Imagine you are a person in one of these stories. Write a conversation with another person from one of the other stories about the ghosts that you have seen.

41 Why are ghost stories popular do you think? What does their popularity tell us about people all round the world? Write your opinion.

Answers for the Activities in this book are available from the Penguin Readers website. A free Activity Worksheet is also available from the website. Activity Worksheets are part of the Penguin Teacher Support Programme, which also includes Progress Tests and Graded Reader Guidelines. For more information, please visit: www.penguinreaders.com.

WORD LIST

appear (v) to come into view; the opposite of **disappear**

army (n) a very large group of soldiers for fighting on land

ashamed (adj) feeling bad because you have done a bad thing

banknote (n) a piece of paper money

cash (n/v) money that you can touch or hold in your hand; to *cash a cheque* means to give a cheque and receive cash for it

cashier (n) a person in a shop or bank who receives and pays out cash to customers

Christmas Eve (n) the day before Christmas

coin (n) a piece of money that is made of metal

confused (adj) not understanding something because of mixed ideas or information

control (v) to make a person do what you want

ghost (n) the form of a dead person that some people believe they can see

hell (n) the place where, in some religions, bad people go after death

moth (n) small things that fly at night, often around bright lights

nephew (n) the son of your brother or sister

odd (adj) surprisingly unusual

scar (n) a line or other shape on the skin from an old cut

servant (n) a person who lives in another person's house and works for them

shade (n) an area that is darker because the sun can't reach it

warn (v) tell someone about a future danger

whisper (v) speak very quietly so that other people can't hear

The Black Cat and Other Stories
Edgar Allan Poe

Are you brave enough to read four of Poe's famous horror stories?
Edgar Allan Poe wrote strange stories about terrible people and
evil crimes. Don't read this book late at night!

Stories from Shakespeare

These are the stories of some of Shakespeare's most famous
plays. We travel to Venice, Greece, Denmark and Rome, and meet
many different people. There is a greedy money-lender, a fairy
king and queen, some Roman politicians and a young prince who
meets the ghost of his murdered father.

The Thirty-nine Steps
John Buchan

A man is killed in Richard Hannay's home. Before his death he
tells Hannay a dangerous secret. Now Hannay's life is in danger.
Who are his enemies and what are they trying to do? And how will
he solve the mystery of 'the thirty-nine steps'?

*There are hundreds of Penguin Readers to choose from – world classics,
film adaptations, modern-day crime and adventure, short stories,
biographies, American classics, non-fiction, plays ...*

For a complete list of all Penguin Readers titles, please contact your local
Pearson Longman office or visit our website.

The Turn of the Screw
Henry James

A young woman comes to a big house to teach two young children. It's her first job and she wants to do it well. But she begins to see strange things – the ghosts of dead people. Do the ghosts want the children?

A Scandal in Bohemia
Sir Arthur Conan Doyle

All kinds of people, from shopkeepers to kings, want the help of Sherlock Holmes in these six stories about the adventures of the famous detective. Who put a diamond in a chicken? Why is there a club for men with red hair? How did the man at the lake die? Can Sherlock Holmes solve the mysteries?

Dracula
Bram Stoker

Count Dracula is a vampire. He drinks people's blood. He lives in a lonely castle in the mountains of Transylvania. But then he comes to England and strange things start happening. People change. People become ill. Professor Van Helsing knows about vampires, but can he stop Count Dracula?

There are hundreds of Penguin Readers to choose from – world classics, film adaptations, modern-day crime and adventure, short stories, biographies, American classics, non-fiction, plays ...

For a complete list of all Penguin Readers titles, please contact your local Pearson Longman office or visit our website.

Longman Dictionaries

Express yourself with confidence!

Longman has led the way in ELT dictionaries since 1935. We constantly talk to students and teachers around the world to find out what they need from a learner's dictionary.

Why choose a Longman dictionary?

Easy to understand

Longman invented the Defining Vocabulary – 2000 of the most common words which are used to write the definitions in our dictionaries. So Longman definitions are always clear and easy to understand.

Real, natural English

All Longman dictionaries contain natural examples taken from real-life that help explain the meaning of a word and show you how to use it in context.

Avoid common mistakes

Longman dictionaries are written specially for learners, and we make sure that you get all the help you need to avoid common mistakes. We analyse typical learners' mistakes and include notes on how to avoid them.

Innovative CD-ROMs

Longman are leaders in dictionary CD-ROM innovation. Did you know that a dictionary CD-ROM includes features to help improve your pronunciation, help you practice for exams and improve your writing skills?

For details of all Longman dictionaries, and to choose the one that's right for you, visit our website:

www.longman.com/dictionaries